From Broke
to
Six Figures

From Broke
to
Six Figures

Steps to Success
in Business and Life

Francis P. "Frank" Lehane

IMPACT DRIVEN▶
PUBLISHING

Published by
Impact Driven Publishing
3129 S. Hacienda Boulevard, Suite #658
Hacienda Heights, CA 91745

Manufactured in the United States of America, or in the United Kingdom when distributed elsewhere.

Lehane, Francis P.
From Broke to Six Figures: Steps to Success in Business and Life
LCCN: 2020907276
ISBN: 978-1-7347528-4-7
eBook: 978-1-7347528-5-4

Interviews and Copy Drafts by: Annie Margis
Cover design by: Joe Potter
Copyediting by: Lara Kennedy
Interior design by: Medlar Publishing Solutions Pvt Ltd., India
Author Photo by: Michael Fireborn
Brand Logo and QR Codes by: Aberlewest Design & Marketing

Francis "Frank" Lehane Brand Vision & Language by: *RichBrands*

www.YourMoneysPower.com

Acknowledgments

Deciding to write a book is one thing. Actually writing one is quite a different experience.

In either case, I decided long ago that if I were to ever write a book, I would never forget the host of people to thank and acknowledge for their contributions to my growth throughout the years.

First, I thank my Lord and Savior Jesus Christ; without His faithfulness and leading, no book or business would have ever been possible.

Second, I thank my loving wife of twenty-nine years, Kathy, who supported our family in the early—and not-so-early—days of my business. It was her faith in me that kept me going, especially when I could not see the light at the end of the tunnel.

I thank for their generosity and willingness my associates and friends Peter Kitzerow, Tom Love, Emily Prendiville, and the other dedicated professionals in the Breakaway League, as well as Michael Doherty, who introduced me to Tom Love.

Last but not least are the behind-the-scenes branding, marketing, and writing professionals Rich Kozak and Annie Margis. Without their support and painstaking guidance, this book would have only been a dream unfulfilled. Thank you all!

Table of Contents

Foreword:
From Broke to Six Figures

I've always dreamed of making a difference in the world, to have my life count for something.

I've finally figured out how to do it.

When I was a kid, I never had a very high opinion of my own abilities and intellect. I almost didn't graduate from junior high. Many people close to me don't know that, because I was ashamed of it. As a high school fresh-man, I was afraid of anyone finding out I was in "special" classes my first semester. In my senior year, I took a lot of college prep classes and even higher math like algebra because I wanted to prove to my parents and siblings I could get into college.

We've all heard it before, haven't we? "Go to college. A brand-name one if possible. Major in something useful, not basket-weaving. Get good grades. Be smarter than the next student. Know how to market yourself better than the next person."

I did what I was told and went to college. Five years later, with my French degree in hand, I set out—like so many others—to be successful. I soon realized that what I had a passion for in college was unmarketable in the real world, unless I wanted to wait tables in a French restaurant.

What confidence I had built by enduring five years of disciplined and often grueling study crumbled with the fear that what all the know-betters had told me was true: "You wasted five years in college."

In 1983, I got a job in the booming aerospace industry. I thought to myself, *Wow! I've arrived!* But the future held more for me than I could have imagined.

In night school, I trained hard to be a design draftsman. But after several years designing oil refineries, I realized I wasn't making the difference that I dreamed of making.

The Discipline of Self-Development

After suffering three layoffs from various jobs, I was no nearer to making any kind of difference in the world.

I knew I needed to become *the person I needed to be* to make the difference I wanted to make, so I spent thousands of dollars and over five years of my life taking every self-development course I could find.

Fast forward to 1994.

How I Got into Financial Services

I remember sharing my first-ever vision statement in front of 200+ fellow participants in one of my self-development training courses. One man complimented me, saying, "Hey, I heard your vision statement, and there's an opportunity you'd be great at." He told me about a huge financial services company willing to train people like me—in a field I knew nothing about. The man said, "I know you hate your job. Come with me to check this company out."

I was so desperate to change what I was doing in my life that I threw myself into this new opportunity with the excitement a kid feels on Christmas Day. I saw it as a way I could make the huge and lasting difference in people's lives I'd always dreamed of making. And I wouldn't even have to go back to college and get another degree to do it.

I hit the books like I had in college and passed all the state licensing exams. *Hurray!* I thought. *Now I have my chance to make a difference!* With my newfound knowledge, I enthusiastically shared my sales presentations with friends and family, who listened patiently.

So began my part-time career selling life insurance and mutual funds. Learning how financial products worked was the easy part. The hard part was recruiting a salesforce that would make sales. My newfound career quickly became a nightmare. I soon realized that getting people to sell anything was like herding cats:

almost impossible, especially if they suspected they were working for you and that you were getting paid more than they were.

At this time I suffered what I decided was my last layoff from corporate America. I saw this as my opportunity to go full-time in learning how to change people's lives through the financial services industry.

The Rough Years

Now began years of setbacks and failure. I was not even making a living. I was happy that my wife had a full-time job and was willing to support us, especially after I spent all of my 401K and savings. I still tell people she always had more faith than I did in what I was doing. Every time I felt like looking for a paying job, she said, "You're having some success. You just need to do more."

Much of my lack of success was due to the fact that I didn't have what the sales profession calls *killer instinct*. It wasn't that I didn't believe in the goodness and significance of what I was doing. I was afraid of hearing "No!" and being rejected, of being embarrassed. My ego would stop me whenever I heard a "No!" or someone said something that caused me to doubt my motives.

The following negatives I heard about sales and selling crept into my brain:

- Nobody likes salespeople.
- Nobody wants to be sold.
- Salespeople don't really care what they sell. They just care about making money.
- Insurance is a necessary evil. It's a gamble. It's a scam.
- Why don't you get a real job?

What? Me, a scammer? Get a *real* job?

My eyes were eventually opened to the reality that a multilevel marketing company is more interested in attracting people who can supply warm prospective clients to sell products to than in educating them about the pitfalls and challenges ahead.

Disappointed and discouraged, I quit the company after seven years of struggling. But unlike many who got licensed only to quit the business forever, I never quit. Why? Because I believed it could make a big difference in people's lives. In 2003, I discovered real freedom by becoming an independent agent. I was now my own boss.

Health Scare

But years of failure were starting to wear me down. I gained a lot of weight—I weighed almost 290 pounds—and soon afterward I was diagnosed with type 2 diabetes. I was scared. The worst health risk

I'd ever had before was a bad case of the flu. This was serious! I was on a five-medication regimen and had to use a Bi-PAP machine, because in addition to diabetes, I had sleep apnea.

It was then that I made a decision to get my health back. I didn't want to die without making a difference in people's lives! So in spite of the cost, I spent seven thousand dollars and eighteen months on getting healthier. The weight loss people made me their poster child when I lost over one hundred pounds. My doctor gradually took me off of all five diabetes medications. Even my sleep apnea people said I no longer needed the Bi-PAP machine to breathe. I was really making progress, and my confidence soared too.

Finding My *Why*

People don't buy what you do. They buy *why* you do it. But how many of us make time to discover our true motivation for *why* we do what we do in life?

People don't buy what you do. They buy *why* you do it.

In the midst of my failure, I asked myself, "Why am I even in this industry, considering all the effort I put forth over the years for so little return? Of all the opportunities out there, why do I do this? Obviously, there's something about it that keeps me doing it. Otherwise, I would have taken a civil service exam and got up and gone to the post office for a more-or-less guaranteed paycheck years ago."

For years, I knew that why I did what I did couldn't be about the money, because for most of my twenty-four-year career, I made very little of it! No, the reason I chose this career was way bigger than money.

I started asking all kinds of successful people *why* they got into their business and what they did to succeed. I picked their brains. I took all kinds of notes about notions and concepts that I had never been exposed to before.

I became encouraged. If they succeeded, so could I!

I could make a difference in people's lives! I discovered my *why*:

- I help relieve people's emotional discomfort around dealing with their money, which is a major stress factor.
- I clarify the confusion people have around understanding money.
- I help people to protect & multiply their wealth.
- I help people retire years sooner than they think they can.

I realized that *why* I do what I do has very little to do with *what* I could get out of it. My *why* has everything to do with *people* and the difference I make in their lives. I give credit for this one life-changing revelation to a man I met in March 2016, Simon Sinek. Since then, I have viewed Simon's eighteen-minute TED Talk on YouTube over forty times. Each time I see it, I hear something new.

Finally Making a Living

By 2013, I was encouraged by the fact that I was starting to finally make a living in business. By making a living, I mean I was making more than $50,000 a year for the first time ever!

I know that success isn't all about how much money one makes, but money is a good metric to measure success, and I was starting to feel unsuccessful.

I will always remember Rick Itzkowich, a business coach I hired back in 2003, shouting in my face, saying, "What's your problem, Lehane!? There are people in your job who are half as bright as you, with nowhere near the passion you have to really help people, who are making $250,000 a year!"

I've come a long, long way since then. I now realize that all the trials and failures I went through prepared me for what was about to happen in September 2016.

2016—Remembering Stuff I Used to Know

In 2016, I met a man, now a good friend, named Tom Love. Tom began teaching me—no, he began *reminding* me about stuff I already knew, things I was taught years ago. One thing he said, which I will never forget, was, "Frank, you're about to get a pay raise. It will be effective when you are."

When I started applying Tom's reminders to business and life, people said things to me like, "You're really listening to me! You understand what I want, Frank! I've never had a conversation about my finances like this before. I'm so used to salespeople only wanting to pry more money out of my pocket and sell me more investments. But not you. I feel like you have my back. You are *for* me. This is *fun!*"

So I began to stop selling and start really listening to people.

2017—Success!

Tom's prediction came true. From January to July 2017, I created the largest tax liability for myself (a happy thing) that I or anyone in my family tree had ever had. By July 2017, I had been paid close to $400,000. I don't say that to impress people. I finally understood how finding out what people really want, in a simple yet intentional conversation, and having something valuable to share could make a huge difference in people's lives and a zero-to-six-figure difference in mine.

My wife and I were finally able to buy a new home, after renting for twenty-two years. We paid off over $52,000 in credit card debt, half of which we'd had since we were married in 1990. But much better than all these blessings was the tenfold increase in value and service I was able to render to the people I helped.

Tom Love's reminders had a lot to do with my success. But I also had to change as a person. I had to submit to the reminders and stop trying to be just the bubbly bonehead who wanted everyone to like and accept me.

Once I learned these things, I went from broke to six figures and found success in business and in life. Wow, what a great book title!

Today I serve as **A Saver's Wealth Advocate** (see the details in chapter 6), and I created a company called **SAFE SAVINGS OPTIONS: Using Your Money's Power.**

I'm celebrating my twenty-fourth full year in business, and I've never been so encouraged or had as much fun, simply because of a few life-changing ideas I've learned and applied. I thank God for the special people inside and outside of my industry who taught me the valuable lessons I'm privileged to share with you here in this book and in my online videos.

So what are some of the things I've learned? One of the first life-changing lessons was how to get over my fear of people, which happens to be the subject of chapter 1.

☼ ☼ ☼

Next chapter:
How to overcome your fear.

Is Fear Blocking *Your* Success?

When I was growing up, those closest to me always vocalized their doubts about my intelligence, about my capabilities, and especially about my motives for doing anything. Because of this, I developed the idea that I needed to know everything and know it like an expert, which made me a good conversationalist on many topics.

For as long as I can remember, I've liked to talk, especially if it's about food or airplanes or anything French. Corner me and my foodie sister Diane together, and you'll hear hours of great eating and cooking how-tos. Get another airplane enthusiast together with me in a room, and it's all about the history of flight, from Da Vinci to the space plane. French? Connect me up with a native Francophone, and you'll think you're in a François Truffaut movie.

I have always been comfortable and talkative in familiar settings. But put me in an unfamiliar setting, and I freak out on the inside. Challenge me to engage a stranger, and

I become speechless. Not at all confident or courageous. Introverted to the max.

Throughout my life, I struggled with a fear of asking questions of people who I thought might be smarter or more gifted or successful than me. Years into adulthood, I realized my pride and ego played a big part in fostering this fear.

I struggled with a fear of asking questions of people who I thought might be smarter or more successful than me.

One day, when I shared my fear of starting meaningful conversations with people I don't know and how this fear had stopped me from succeeding for years, a high-powered Fortune 500 attorney friend of mine, Bo Segers, offered me a gem.

Bo said, "People are afraid to talk to people because they fear what people will say to them. They blow it all out of proportion. If you have this fear, relax. Take a tally of the worst things anyone has ever said to you. You might be surprised to learn that these worst things really weren't so bad after all."

Bo went on, "Frank, you take what people say to you, good or bad, too personally. You've programmed yourself to believe that what people say to you is *all about you*."

Bo reminded me that when I ask people questions, their feedback is *not* about me, the asker! Wow, what a concept! For years I was stopped because I believed that people's feedback meant something about me! Me! My goals. My results. My agenda. Me! My! Mine! Crazy, huh?

So I started asking people about themselves. Nothing scary about that. I would only talk about myself if they asked me, "Hey, what do you do?" And even then I had to be on my guard so I wouldn't get back into my old mindset of "me, my, mine."

❖   ❖   ❖

Now that you've learned how to ask people about themselves in order to get rid of fear, learn how *not* to talk to them in chapter 2.

💡 The Frank Spotlight

On Overcoming Fear

❯ Go To

YourMoneysPower.com/OvercomingFear

How *Not* to Talk to People

Business trainers taught me to think that because I knew more than my prospective clients, this gave me a kind of superiority over them.

Therefore, if people wanted to succeed or get what they wanted, they needed me:

- They needed to listen to me.
- They needed to do what I told them to do.

- They needed my life-changing products and services.

Why, then, were people *not* taking me up on my offers to save them?

When I watched myself selling on video, I began to realize I had an awful habit of interrupting people and finishing their sentences. That was turning people off. I was being perceived as someone who thought he had something more important to say than what other people had.

I realized I was talking *at* people. I wasn't engaging people, talking *with* them.

Having Something to Say versus Having Someone to Say It To

Throughout my twenty-odd years in business, I was always taught to go out and find someone, *anyone*, to say something pithy and clever to in order to get them to buy what I was selling. I never thought about actually having something *of value* to say to the person, something that resonated with what *they* wanted instead of what *I* knew was good for them. However, having something *of value* to say versus merely having someone to say it to—this was a major breakthrough, an *aha!* moment.

I had to change. And fast!

When I started listening to people in order to understand what they were saying—to understand what they wanted—life started yielding results I had never got before. Life became easier. Business started being fun.

People began to have conversations with me that meant something to *them* instead of having conversations about *my* agenda.

Without shame and without anxiety, I now have conversations like friends have with friends. I no longer feel I have to prove something or convince anybody of anything. I just need to listen for their concerns and ask them if they want to fix the **Problem** (see chapter 8) causing their concerns.

Never Call the Baby Ugly

This young guy owned a fashion shop in West Hollywood back in the nineties, when I first got into financial services. We got together, and after I did my spiel, he said something that changed my life: "Frank, you're very intelligent, and I like you a lot. But I gotta tell you: Never tell somebody that what they're doing is wrong, that their financial decisions are wrong. When you said that to me, it hurt my feelings, because you don't know how much time and stress and energy I put into it. I'm not going to do business with you, even if you've got manna from heaven. You really ticked me off. And I just wanna let you know, if you want to succeed, you can't do that."

In a couple of words, he shattered my confidence. I felt so embarrassed, because I knew he was right. I'd been trained to tell people that what they were doing was stupid: "I know the right way, and you need to listen to me. I'm the one with the license. I'm gonna fix everything up for you, because apparently you have been unable to figure it out on your own. If you don't listen to me, then you are stupid." With my demeanor and language, that was the message I had been sending.

Ever since that day, I've always remembered that lesson: Don't ever call somebody's baby ugly.

✿   ✿   ✿

In the next chapter:
Learn how to listen to people.

💡 **The Frank Spotlight**

On How *Not* to Talk to People

❯ **Go To**

YourMoneysPower.com/HowNotToTalkToPeople

CHAPTER 3

Listening to Understand

There's nothing worse than giving a long sales spiel on common questions and concerns only to have your prospect say, "Yeah, but that wasn't my question." Once, I told somebody I could absolutely help them save money for their kid's college, only to have them tell me at the end of my presentation, "Yeah, but I don't have any kids."

I used to be so caught up in my head, trying to think of the next smart thing to say, that I'd completely miss what someone was saying to me, and I ended up answering questions they hadn't even asked, answering objections that they didn't even have until I brought them up. All simply because I was not listening to understand; I was listening to respond. I was afraid that if I stopped talking, people might ask me things I didn't know. I thought I needed to have the answers to everything, and I don't.

As kids, we were taught to listen in order to respond to questions. That's not the only—or the best— way to listen.

I discovered that I had to become *way* better at **listening to**

understand people rather than listening to respond. When I first tried this, people were surprised. They would say, "Really? Wait a minute. What did you mean by that? Tell me more."

Tell. Me. More. That was music to my ears!

Tell. Me. More. That was music to my ears!

That's what I'd always wanted people to say! Real communication was finally happening. My words were striking chords, resonating with the questions people were already asking themselves about problems *they* were interested in solving.

Listening to understand, along with some other ideas I'm going to tell you about, made it possible for me to go from zero to six figures in my business.

⚙   ⚙   ⚙

Next chapter:
Wants versus needs.

♀ The Frank Spotlight

On Listening to Understand

❯ Go To

YourMoneysPower.com/ListeningToUnderstand

CHAPTER 4

Wants versus Needs

For more than twenty years of my career, I—and everybody else in the financial industry—was trained to convince you that you need things.

You NEED to get out of debt.
You NEED to plan for retirement.
You NEED to buy life insurance.
You NEED some investments.

You need a jacket to go outside. You need to eat better. You need a job. You need to take a bath.

Don't you just love other people telling you what you need?

People say, "Yeah, I might need all those things," yet they don't take action. Why? Because in their experience, whenever they hear the word *need*, it sends a jolt to the part of the brain that deals with things that cost money, and their experience tells them it costs money every time they *need* something.

So instead of focusing on needs, I talk with people about their *wants*. My objective? Finding ways people can get what they want.

My objective? Finding ways people can get what they want.

I love finding ways people can get what they want.

For example, I say something like, "If I could show you in black and white, with paper and pencil, how to move your taxable savings into nontaxable accounts, where it could grow and be protected, and spend like there's three times as much money in there, without risk of losing it, would you want me to show you how to do that using money you're *already spending*?"

People say, "I want that! That is for me! I want to pay less in taxes.

I want to start saving, growing, and protecting some real money!"

Ever since I started having conversations focused on wants versus needs, I've noticed that people have started chasing me, saying, "Can you show me how much of my savings I can grow and protect? How soon can I get started doing this?"

I can't tell you how many times I've seen the joy and relief in people's eyes when they learn ideas they never knew before so that now they can achieve what they once thought would be impossible.

Many people struggle all their lives simply to afford the things they need, like food and shelter and health care. When people's needs are met, they can turn their focus to things they want. "Yeah, I got a house; I got a car; I got a good job; I got some money in the bank. Now what do I want? I want to learn to play the guitar. I want to learn how to paint watercolors like Bob Ross."

Maybe they dream of donating their time and energy to causes they feel strongly about, maybe of taking trips to far-off lands. Maybe they hope to adopt children because they could never have any.

Make a list of things you really want. At this point, you might feel ashamed a little bit of writing down some things because they're too out-landish, or even selfish. You may feel that if you mention the things you really want in life—like world peace, the eradication of disease and starvation, whiter teeth—you're going to be seen in your circle of friends as overly optimistic, if not worse.

But that's where life begins: when people actually get what they want. Life isn't made up of merely surviving to feed yourself.

Imagine getting things you really want. The emotions around getting those things you want are completely different from the deep motivations around getting the things you need. How did you feel when you read "play the guitar" and "paint watercolors"? Happier than when you read "food, clothing, and health care," I bet.

✵ ✵ ✵

In the next chapter, you'll learn how to stop selling!

♀ The Frank Spotlight

On Wants versus Needs

❯ Go To

YourMoneysPower.com/WantsVersusNeeds

CHAPTER 5

Stop Selling! Just Stop It!

Many salespeople are not very successful because they can't stop talking long enough to really listen to people. They work very hard with little to show for it. And a lot of the reason why is this: they *can't stop selling*. I don't mean stop *making* sales. Somewhere, a sale must be made. That's business! No, what I mean is they can't stop "pitching" the sale.

You've seen this happen in your encounters with cell phone salespeople or real estate agents. They begin by talking. And they talk and talk and talk. When they're not talking, they're thinking of how they can rebut your objections or respond to your questions, with the ever-present specter looming of *closing* you on all the benefits and features, all the bells and whistles, all the blah blah blah you need like a runaway firehose.

And if you ever say "No" to a sales rep, you know what happens next.

It turns into a battle of wills. They start selling harder and harder, and they tick you off more and more, until you feel bad on the inside.

Even if you're sitting there with a smile on your face, nodding, you're thinking, "This is why I hate talking to salespeople."

Salespeople succeed or fail based on how many sales they make. In this life-or-death struggle, they are taught to use many tactics. They cozy up to you. They try to build rapport. They try to get you to like them and believe them so you'll buy something from them.

Remember the films *Boiler Room* and *Glengarry Glen Ross*? There's a lot of truth about the lives of salespeople in those movies. I've known sales managers like the character portrayed by Alec Baldwin. They are scary. Nightmare material.

I hasten to remind people that for most of my career, I was "selling" like my life depended on it. And anyone who knew me then would tell you I acted and sounded like my life depended on it too. It wasn't a pretty sight on either end of the table. I realized this after listening to recordings and watching videos of myself in action.

Stop selling? Why do salespeople look at me like I just landed in a spaceship when I say this? In their minds, this concept is a major paradigm shift, a major obstacle to overcome if they ever want to go from zero to six figures. But what do I mean when I say, "Stop selling?" What did I start doing instead of selling that catapulted me from mediocrity to success?

What did I start doing instead of selling that catapulted me from mediocrity to success?

Shut Up!

My good friend Andy White introduced me to the idea of "shutting up." That's right, shutting up. Take a breath. Pause. Consider what the other person is saying. Give thoughtful responses based on what they say. Ask for clarification if necessary.

Andy shared with me how he tried this when he took the kids out for ice cream. He said to the waitress serving them, "You probably realize that our leaders, regardless of which party, pay less in taxes than you and I and all of our cousins combined. How does that make you feel?"

She said, "That really chaps my hide!"

Then Andy asked the waitress, "If there was a way for you to do what they do to pay less in taxes legally and ethically to benefit yourself, would you want to learn that?"

"Yeah!" the waitress blurted out with enthusiasm.

Then Andy said, "Well, that's what I do. Jot down your information in my notebook, and someone in the office will contact you next week."

Then he shut up and got busy eating ice cream.

In my earlier days, a person I hold in high esteem asked me, "How come your appointments are three hours long, Frank? They should be no longer than forty-five minutes to maybe an hour. So why do you take two and a half hours? Because you can't shut up, that's why. People said 'Yes' forty-five minutes ago, and here you are, blah blah blah blah blah. Man, take a pill."

Right about early 2015, I had still not broken the surface in my business after, gosh, twenty years in my industry. I thought I was doing pretty good making about $50,000 a year.

But if you know anything about what top earners make in the financial industry, you know that's barely scratching the tip of the iceberg.

I realized that if I couldn't make a living in this business, then I didn't have a business. And if I was not effective in business, I wouldn't be *in* business very long.

But wait! There's more!

After listening to recordings of myself in action in the early part of my career, I was so embarrassed, shocked! I almost couldn't bear to hear myself. I was interrupting people incessantly. I was finishing their sentences. I was riding completely roughshod over what they were telling me. I wasn't even present in what I was doing. I was going on autopilot.

I said to myself, "Frank, you just need to shut up. You don't let these people say anything. What is the matter with you?"

I knew what was the matter with me: I was terribly anxious, because I had based my whole idea of success in life and my self-worth on everybody getting involved with what I was doing. When I actually became conscious of it, my life changed for the better.

After I shared this story during one of our calls, salespeople in my organization came up to me and said, "I see things more clearly now. I no longer fear getting criticism, because I have something to contribute, and I don't really care what you think about me."

Financial salespeople are taught to walk around the neighborhoods that they have been told have a lot of high-net-worth individuals and go door-knocking to sell things. I did it.

Every Monday morning, our sales manager would say, "This is the stock that you should sell this week. Here are the specifics of it: now study it and get out there and sell it."

That's what I did. I walked around this pretty affluent neighborhood, and I knocked on this door where a very old lady lived. This lady was ancient. She'd never been married. I started my little pitch, and she interrupted, "Well, I want to buy me some municipal bonds."

I couldn't believe it! Here I'd been sweating my butt off in my suit on a sunny day, and everybody's either not home or they're slamming the door in my face. And this lady actually wants to buy municipal bonds! So I sold her five thousand dollars' worth.

I went over there one day several months later to visit her, and she wasn't there. I learned she had been moved over to a fairly nice old folks home.

Good friends of hers were clearing out her house. And the guy got up and got in my face, and he said, "Wait a minute! Are you that Edward Jones guy?"

I thought, *How does this guy know what I do?*

I said, "Yeah, that's me."

He says to the other people, "Here's the snake that sold our friend thirty-year maturity municipal bonds she'll never live to spend."

I got angry inside. I got angry because I knew that he was right. I had—unknowingly—been a snake.

In my own defense, I was ignorant. I was a salesperson charged with selling things, and this lady didn't need any convincing. She said, "Man, that's a great rate." But the only reason she could get a higher rate of return was because of the lengthy maturity date.

I'm so glad that she just bought the minimum amount you could buy, a measly little five thousand, because people buy these things by the hundreds of thousands.

I said to myself, "Man! That's the problem with being a salesperson. A Saver's Wealth Advocate would never have done that."

Since I quit "selling," people say to me, "We've never had a conversation with a financial person like you before, where we feel like you are really listening to us, where we feel heard. We truly feel you are *for* us, on our side. We don't feel like we're being sold."

⚙   ⚙   ⚙

Next chapter:

How can you tell the difference between an ordinary financial services salesperson and A Saver's Wealth Advocate?

💡 **The Frank Spotlight**

On Stopping Selling

❯ **Go To**

YourMoneysPower.com/StoppingSelling

CHAPTER 6

A Salesperson? Or A Saver's Wealth Advocate?

I believe that financial salespeople are not interested in helping you understand how money really works as much as they just want you to buy their products and services. People laugh when I say that—because they know it's true.

As **A Saver's Wealth Advocate**, I serve by sharing with you things you need to know. I love the fact that this makes me stand out from the dozens of financial advisors you could find within a mile radius of where you live.

A financial salesperson is more intent on selling you a product, while A Saver's Wealth Advocate is more intent on having you understand *why* and what the consequences are going to be later in life, when you want to take and spend your money. Are you going to lose it? Are you going to get taxed to death? You're going to have to pay commissions again on the way out. What are the ramifications? Salespeople, for the most part, don't focus on that.

Many financial advisors are lower-middle-income people with a job and a neat title that says, "I know more than you do, and I'm going to tell you how to get wealthy." Any number of financial salespeople are eager to sell you products you *need* to buy, versus wanting you to know the consequences of what you do with your money.

Recall your own experiences dealing with financial salespeople. They begin an almost endless listing of all the benefits and features, all the bells and whistles, all the blah blah blah *they think you need*. And when they don't succeed in selling you their plan or product, they think it's *you* who is the problem.

If you've ever said "No" to a salesperson, you know what I mean. Many salespeople just keep trying to convince you and to prove what they say is true: you *need* what they're selling. They might even get angry!

Then you get more and more annoyed. Even though you may be sitting there with a smile on your face and nodding your head in the affirmative, you're really thinking, *How can I save face and get out of this situation?*

The salesperson, on the other hand, thinks your smile and nod mean, "Ooh, tell me more!" *Not.*

Here's a make-believe conversation you might have with a financial services rep:

Rep: You need to buy some XYZ from me.

You: Why?

Rep: Because they're good, and you need them.

You: Are you buying XYZ for yourself?

Rep: Well, no.

You: Then why are you asking me to buy XYZ from you?

Rep: Because that's what my boss told me to sell.

Maybe you've had conversations like that!

I was trained to be a salesman for most of my career. But now I'm A Saver's Wealth Advocate. The difference between a salesperson and an advocate is that a salesperson sells products that they're told by their company to sell, products they may or may not believe in. An advocate is somebody who sits with you and works toward solving your **Problem** in partnership with you.

As A Saver's Wealth Advocate, I serve by educating people on how to protect their savings and multiply the growth of their wealth by avoiding erosive fees, expenses, and taxes. Now they can achieve financial goals they never believed they could reach. It is my mission to educate, take a stand, and advocate for people who want to protect & multiply their wealth. These are people who would otherwise have their wealth taken from them, simply because no one took the time to educate them in how to effectively steward their own wealth. Achieving these goals is a process.

As A Saver's Wealth Advocate, it is my mission to educate, take a stand, and advocate for people who want to protect & multiply their wealth.

A Saver's Wealth Advocate does not go door-knocking. A Saver's Wealth Advocate does not give sales pitches. A Saver's Wealth Advocate looks at the entire situation that a person is in and listens empathetically to what they really want to do, the direction they want to take, and what they want to have happen.

And if the person asks A Saver's Wealth Advocate to do things that are completely outside their broad area of expertise, they do not change up and say, "Oh gosh. I better start selling that stuff too!" What they *do* say is, "Let's stay focused on this proven, time-honored legal strategy for protecting & multiplying wealth that we *know* works and *ensures* that you meet your financial goals. It is our area of deep expertise, and this is what I am personally committed to helping you with. Let's choose to not get off track by chasing a specific 'product opportunity' outside of the strategy." So you see, there's a significant difference between the behavior of a financial salesperson and the heart of A Saver's Wealth Advocate.

As A Saver's Wealth Advocate, I approach every person I encounter with a servant's heart, putting their desires and needs first.

As A Saver's Wealth Advocate, I help people release their dread and anxiety around money.

As A Saver's Wealth Advocate, I listen carefully to an individual's history of past mistakes, disappointments, and pitfalls.

As A Saver's Wealth Advocate, I can help a person increase family time and vacations and create exciting retirement activities.

Uncommon Questions and Surprising Answers

You may never have heard of A Saver's Wealth Advocate before, so here are some answers to questions you may have:

You: Are there specific types of people who can benefit the most by learning from A Saver's Wealth Advocate?

Me: Absolutely. They are the people determined to be millionaires, not loser-naires.

You: What skills are required for being A Saver's Wealth Advocate?

Me: Several, but these are the Big Three:
- Empathetic listener
- Patient educator
- Expert on the finance of savings

You: Who is most effective at being A Saver's Wealth Advocate?

Me: Someone perceptive in hearing your needs and fears and lots more . . .

You: What top-level impact can A Saver's Wealth Advocate have on Future Millionaires?

Me: It begins by turning your liabilities into assets and goes up from there.

You: How can I identify a financial professional as being A Saver's Wealth Advocate?

Me: If a financial profesional asks you how much money you can afford to risk losing, they are *not* A Saver's Wealth Advocate.

You: What questions will A Saver's Wealth Advocate ask me?

Me: A Saver's Wealth Advocate carefully listens to you as you answer the eleven questions asked during a *Safe Saver's Questionnaire Consult*.

You: Can I have more spendable wealth when I retire?

Me: Yes. A Saver's Wealth Advocate can show you that *where* your money is sitting is more important than what it could earn there, as well as how to keep more of it after taxes.

You: Can my beliefs around money prevent me from multiplying my savings?

Me: Yes. Particularly if you don't know what you don't know.

You: What should a committed and prudent Safe Saver look for in a financial advisor?

Me: First, look for whether they are A Saver's Wealth Advocate, and then after they have listened empathetically to clearly understand you and your family's situation, listen for how they *only* recommend what is in your best interest.

You: Are there *Safe* Savings Options that do not put my money at risk?

Me: Yes, and you can learn how to multiply those savings from A Saver's Wealth Advocate.

Over the past twenty-four years, I went from being a pipeline draftsman to becoming A Saver's Wealth Advocate making a difference in people's lives. It was a long journey that continues even today. Along the way, I came to know the real reason *why* I chose my particular industry to make the difference I yearned to make for people.

I love the story of the *Wizard of Oz*, especially the part where Toto and Dorothy and the Tin Man and the Scarecrow and the Lion have finally made it into the Emerald City to have an audience with Oz.

While Dorothy and the others quake in their boots at the thunderous flaming image in front of them, Toto, attracted by a commotion going on behind a nearby curtain, jumps out of Dorothy's arms and races over to reveal what's happening behind the scenes.

It took lovable little Toto to find out the truth that set Dorothy and the others on the path to reach their dreams.

I want to be Toto. I want to pull the curtain back so you can realize your dreams.

I want to be Toto. I want to pull the curtain back so you can realize your dreams.

✿   ✿   ✿

Next chapter:
Your wealth pie.

─────── 💡 **The Frank Spotlight** ───────

On Saver's Wealth Advocate

─────── ❯ **Go To** ───────

YourMoneysPower.com/SaversWealthAdvocate

CHAPTER 7

Your Wealth Pie?
Or Pie in the Sky?

Picture all of your wealth as a pie cut into thirds. No one needs a finance degree to understand two of the three pieces of the pie. Let's call one third of all the wealth you've grown **Accumulated Wealth**—your savings, investments, property, and toys (RV, boat, etc.).

Let's call the next third your **Lifestyle Wealth**—what you earn at your job or business. This is where you go to get the money you need to pay your mortgage, pay taxes, pay bills, and buy groceries.

You take from the Lifestyle piece to put into the Accumulated Wealth piece. You hope this will grow enough so you can afford all your *needs* so that then you can set your sights on someday affording all the things you *want*.

But wait! There's yet another, third piece completing the pie, and many people don't even know what's in that one or how it works.

The financial industry has done a magnificent job helping people focus on pie piece number one, the Accumulated Wealth piece. They underemphasize or ignore the third piece of the pie. Can you even guess what this third piece of pie is?

This third is Transferred Wealth. It represents all the wealth people unknowingly and unnecessarily transfer by giving it away, letting it slip through their hands day by day, week by week, month by month, and year by year in the form of fees, expenses, and taxes to Wall Street, to financial institutions, and to the government. What they thought was a complete pie has become partly pie in the sky.

I began asking myself, "If people could be taught how to recapture for themselves $50,000 of their transferred wealth that they didn't even know they were losing, would they want me to find it for them?"

The answer I got back was an astoundingly unanimous *yes*. Last year, I helped clients re-steward on average $50,000 they were giving away needlessly because of what they were taught by others to do with their wealth. I jumpstarted these family financial leaders into providing a legacy for their children and grandchildren. But it went up from there.

Jumpstart *Your* Wealth Pie

If I could put wealth you'd be otherwise losing back into your hands to use and control, would our relationship be profitable for you?

If you hear yourself saying "Yes!" to that, hold on! My momma told me that if a thing sounds too good to be true, *run away*!

But one of the ideas I was reminded about recently—an idea that catapulted me from zero to six figures—was this:

If a thing looks too good to be true, DIG DEEPER!

Many opportunities I've benefited from sounded too good to be true—at first. So I encourage you to dig deeper. And it's OK to be skeptical. We honor skepticism, without enabling it to turn into disbelief or argument.

Answering Your Questions

Here are some questions about wealth I hear a lot. I've answered them for you.

You: Is it even possible to protect savings dollars and multiply them too?

Me: The wealthiest families know how, but probably no one has shown you.

You: Why do financial advisors always talk about "managing the risk" of losing money?

Me: Some financial advisors expect that you won't mind losing money now and then.

I talk about *avoiding* risk while multiplying your savings.

You: Why do I feel guilty for not investing my hard-earned savings in stocks and bonds like financial planners tell me I should?

Me: The *should* is designed to prompt you to make an immediate product purchase and to feel guilty if you do *not* purchase what they say you *should*. A Saver's Wealth Advocate educates you so you know how to choose what is in *your* best interest. A Saver's Wealth Advocate doesn't use *should*. If you choose to *not* put your money *at risk* by purchasing what they say you should, then you *do not have to feel guilty*.

You: Can my precious savings grow, protected, in the stock market?

Me: Grow? Yes, possibly. Protected? Are you kidding?

You: Are there savings options that are "safe"?

Me: Yes, and Savvy Savers prefer a select few. In many other savings options, "safe" keeps your money from multiplying.

You: Are there specific Safe Savings Options that do *not* put my money *at risk*?

Me: Yes, there absolutely are. However, be careful of

investment advisors who laugh at your question and say anything like, "No pain, no gain; no risk, no profit; now's the time to get in," because they are probably not going to present you with Safe Savings Options.

You: I've been studying my financial advisor's material, but I don't understand: What is diversification?

Me: They teach you to be diversified in your investments in order to "spread the risk to minimize it." Since 2007–2008, many wonder if *diversification* is the investment industry's jargon for "We don't know either."

You: Can my beliefs around money prevent me from multiplying my savings?

Me: Yes, particularly if you don't know what you don't know.

A good friend of mine, Michael Doherty, once told me, "We live in a world made up of 'half-truths,' but a half-truth can be so wide you could drive a Mack truck through it."

Protecting your savings requires a simple decision. Multiplying those savings requires learning a time-honored legal strategy.

I welcome you to stick around long enough to get the whole truth. The whole truth might prevent you from making the mistakes and pit-falls I and many of my esteemed colleagues have made. How good would it be to have the combined wisdom of 135 years of experience at your fingertips?

How good would it be to have the combined wisdom of 135 years of experience at your fingertips?

You've got it.

    ☼   ☼   ☼

Next chapter:
The problem.

 The Frank Spotlight

On The Wealth Pie

 Go To

YourMoneysPower.com/TheWealthPie

CHAPTER 8

Safely Climbing Your Financial Mt. Everest

The **Problem** will impact you in a huge way when you start spending the money you have worked hard all of your working life to save.

Every income-earning person in our country faces the same Problem, regardless of their level of income. The Problem is real, yet it is imperceptible to the majority of people who earn money.

While every Tom, Dick, and Harry financial salesperson wants you to focus on returns and risk and what product you need, my mission is to educate you on an age-old Problem affecting everyone, from the very wealthy to the minimum wage earner.

Risk

You might say, "I'm really afraid of market rates going up, down, up, down, down, down, down." What you don't see that you *really* need to be afraid of are the mandatory taxes that you're going to pay on all of this money that you've done so well to amass.

Many financial advisors encourage people's greed and fear. As insane as it sounds, they teach that without risking your money, growing your money is impossible.

401K

Financial advisors tell you that deferring your taxes in 401Ks or IRAs can "save" you taxes. Has anyone ever showed you the actual numbers in black and white? What you don't know can and will hurt you.

If you believe that our government has a runaway spending habit and that taxes can only go up in the future to support the spending, how can postponing or deferring the inevitable tax bill today help you later, in a higher-than-today tax future?

When you were just starting out in your career, maybe you got a job with a company that offered a 401K or an IRA. You eagerly took it and started putting money in. You were not making that much money, so you were in a very low tax bracket, maybe 20 percent.

The years go by, and you do well in your career and financially, and now you're in a much higher tax bracket, say 30 percent.

At retirement, when you begin to withdraw your savings, you're going to pay taxes in the higher tax bracket, which will negate all the benefits—if there were any—of saving when you were in the lower tax bracket.

What happens to your financial growth? You might have to *give much of it back* to the government. Discovering that problem too late can be prevented early. And preventing that problem early avoids unforeseen negative impacts—specifically on Social Security taxability and Medicare premium increases.

Products Are Not the Solution

Without proper education about the Problem and how to fix it, no product will work. No product will solve the Problem.

An entire industry and even the government are trying to take your attention away from the real Problem: you're going to pay taxes, and if you've succeeded financially, you'll pay more in taxes than someone who didn't succeed.

It's a bigger Problem than it was when you weren't making money.

Doubting Thomases

Some people have wanted me to meet with their current advisor to compare strategies in a friendly and productive environment free of negativity. I stand ready to educate the people I serve, no matter what it takes, and I welcome people's doubts and skepticism.

I want to know your doubts. I want to know your skepticism about what you hear and the way you feel about what I'm telling you. It wasn't that many years ago that I had the same skepticism and doubts. Then I found out the truth. The whole truth.

When I show people their blind spots, they always say, "Wow! You've shown us in such a way that we can see it. We had a feeling that something was off, but we couldn't put a finger on it. Wow! Thank you so much for revealing this. Gosh! I wish I'd known this twenty years ago! Can you fix this Problem? Yes? Will you fix this Problem? Let's get going. Let's fix it."

And that's when the joy of engagement becomes deeper and people start revealing things to me that they've never shared with others, because now they trust me. Now I'm an ally. Now we're partners. I will show them ideas and concepts they need to know, ideas that helped me and the people I serve go from zero to six (or more) figures.

Pick Your Sherpa to Skillfully Guide You

Many people have not learned that the rules and skills for *climbing up* your financial Mt. Everest—amassing of wealth during your highest earning and saving years—work way differently from the rules and skills for *getting safely down* your Mt. Everest—spending your mountain of savings. Knowing the rules and skills for getting safely *down* can be a matter of financial "life and death." I'm not kidding! Let me illustrate what I'm talking about.

Picture yourself camped out at the bottom of Everest, and two Sherpas are standing there to help you get safely to the summit and then safely down.

Sherpa Number One is skilled at getting people to the summit.

Sherpa Number Two is skilled at bringing people safely down.

What if you were only allowed to pick one of these Sherpas?

A lot of people would say, "I want to get to the summit! That's my goal!"

So picture yourself at the summit. You've taken your selfie. Now you need to get safely down. Your trusty Sherpa Number One's skill was getting you to the summit. Sadly, 75 percent of the people who die climbing the real Mount Everest die on the way *down*. They are still there. Frozen solid.

Sherpa Number One represents much of the financial industry's mission. They focus on helping you get to the summit—to amass your wealth.

But now you want to get safely home to brag to everybody, "Hey, look! I climbed up to the top of Mount Everest and planted my flag!"

The Problem

Now here is where the Problem becomes obvious. Remember how we said the rules and skills work very differently on the way down? Many people have not considered what those rules and skills for getting *down* safely are, because they've been taught to put all their focus on getting to the summit. Getting to the summit is a noble ambition, but it's only half the journey. On the way back down, that's where *their financial crisis will become obvious to them.*

So what happens if this Problem goes undetected?

Now, I'm not a fortune teller, but I will predict one thing: when you start spending your retirement savings, not only will you owe taxes on all that tax-deferred money you saved, you will owe a lot *more* taxes at that time than you ever *saved* while your money was growing.

That's the Problem.
You will owe a lot *more* taxes at retirement than you ever *saved* while your money was growing.

Did anyone ever tell you this was going to happen? Now you know.

Is there a **Solution** to the **Problem**? You bet your bottom dollar there is.

☼   ☼   ☼

Up next:
There is a solution.

♀ The Frank Spotlight

On The Problem

❯ Go To

YourMoneysPower.com/TheProblem

CHAPTER 9

Being a Savvy Saver

When an ordinary financial advisor talks to the owner of a pizza shop with annual revenues of $1 million and says, "If I were your advisor and I showed you how you could invest the $200,000 you take home from your million-dollar revenues—after paying taxes, buying pizza dough and pepperoni, and paying rent, insurance, and all the overhead expenses of operating your pizzeria—and I could get you a

10-percent return on that $200,000 (I did the math: that's a $20,000 return), would that make you happy?"

Maybe you'd say, "Yes."

But then you'd think about the *risk* of losing all that money in a shaky market, plus the fees and expenses you'd pay. Now this opportunity doesn't look so good anymore.

By the way, there are probably three hundred financial advisors nearby who talk and think exactly like this—about *your* money.

As A Saver's Wealth Advocate, I would choose to say instead:

"Let's examine the $800,000 you are *already* spending as expenses to generate $1 million of revenues—the taxes, pizza dough, pepperoni, rent, insurance, and *all* those overhead expenses—and uncover ways for you to *lower or eliminate* those expenses by 10 percent on that $800,000 that you are *already* spending (10 percent of $800,000 is $80,000), and let's do that without any risk of market loss and without any additional fees or expenses. Should we do that?"

The pizza shop owner would say, "Yes! Get on over here!"

Why?

Business owners know there are only two ways to make more money:

1. Make more sales
2. Reduce expenses

This is why business owners go nuts every year trying to save money. What if they had someone who could show them their blind spots in areas where they're already spending? Smart business owners know they have little to lose and much to gain from this idea.

Knowing the **Problem** and being concerned enough to fix it is the **Solution**. Knowing how to effectively use the existing tax code is *absolutely key*.

Ask your financial advisor whether they have already solved the Problem for themselves. Tell them to prove it.

Have you ever asked your financial advisor whether they are wealthy?

How wealthy? Should somebody who isn't wealthier than you be advising you on how to get wealthy?

Should somebody who isn't wealthier than you be advising you on how to get wealthy?

A Saver's Wealth Advocate can help you protect and grow your wealth in such a way that your tax liability is either minimized or eliminated, legally. A Saver's Wealth Advocate can help you retire early.

"How?" you ask.

By using the tax code itself.

Would you like to do that?

What I'm talking about is not rocket science. The proven Solution has been used by wealthy American taxpayers for decades to grow and protect wealth and enjoy it.

Banks know and use this strategy. They've been using it for over 150 years. But they're not in business to teach you the strategy. They're not going to say, "Hey, c'mon back behind the curtain, and we'll show you something that will blow your mind." They're not going to do that.

That's why I get to do what I do. I have a wonderful job!

☼　　☼　　☼

Next:
What you do is not why you're here.

⚲ The Frank Spotlight

On Being A Savvy Saver

❯ Go To

YourMoneysPower.com/BeingASavvySaver

CHAPTER 10

What You Do Is Not Why You're Here

Financial **is just the quality that gives your legacy its power.**

Frank Lehane

We're here for a reason. What we leave behind after we're gone, our legacy, speaks to the purpose of why we are here.

Your legacy is not just financial. *Financial* is just the quality that gives your legacy its power. You will leave a legacy of love and a legacy of your spiritual growth and discipleship. You'll leave a legacy of personal energy: the things you've written, the things you've stated, the things that you thought worthy, the things you created. These are things that people know you stand for, things you'll be remembered for. This is your impact legacy.

Using the power of uninterrupted execution on all your legacy elements grows them exponentially.

When you learn about and leverage **Safe Savings Options**, then you structure a financial legacy. You can pass that legacy down in the form of inheritance to your family and your extended family, and you can give it to others through charitable causes.

Caring for others even after you've passed on means making a choice now, not putting off making the choice for a couple years. Caring means focusing on that choice. It means planning and uninterrupted execution.

Financial is Just the Quality that Gives Your Legacy Its Power

Our clients have shared these reviews with us:

- "I like the way these people think. They've got an entrepreneurial mindset like me."
- "They taught me unique tools and skills I'd never heard of, but I wanted and needed to know them."
- "The Mt. Everest metaphor makes total sense. My Saver's Wealth Advocate was the Sherpa who steered me safely and helped me multiply my wealth."

A Saver's Wealth Advocate

- guides you faithfully and with integrity,
- teaches you the rules to create a more impactful financial legacy,

- turns on the lights,
- helps you take your blinders off, and
- empowers you by giving you skills and teaching you how to use them.

Before, maybe you didn't see these opportunities, the ability to protect & multiply wealth for family legacy and charitable giving. Now you can see that those opportunities lie within your grasp.

Let's keep this conversation going.

☼   ☼   ☼